Rookie
Read-About®
Science

The Sun

by Cody Crane

Content Consultant
Kevin Manning
Astronomer

Reading Consultant
Jeanne M. Clidas, Ph.D.
Reading Specialist

Children's Press®
An Imprint of Scholastic Inc.

Library of Congress Cataloging-in-Publication Data
Names: Crane, Cody, author.
Title: The Sun/by Cody Crane.
Other titles: Rookie read-about science.
Description: New York: Children's Press, an imprint
of Scholastic Inc., 2018. | Series: Rookie read-about?
science | Includes index.
Identifiers: LCCN 2017028046| ISBN 9780531230879
(library binding) | ISBN 978-0-531-22983-5 (pbk.)
Subjects: LCSH: Sun—Juvenile literature. | Stars—
Juvenile literature.
Classification: LCC QB521.5 .C73 2018 | DDC
523.7—dc23 LC record available at https://lccn.loc.
gov/2017028046

Produced by Spooky Cheetah Press
Art direction: Tom Carling, Carling Design Inc.
Creative direction: Judith Christ-Lafond for Scholastic

Published in 2018 by Children's Press, an imprint of
Scholastic Inc.

Printed in Heshan, China   62

2 3 4 5 6 7 8 9 10 R 27 26 25 24 23 22 21 20 19 18

Photographs ©: cover Sun: egal/Getty Images; cover
background: Kozachenko Maksym/Shutterstock; back
cover: 751/iStockphoto; cartoon dog throughout: Kelly
Kennedy; 1: SDO/AIA/HMI/Goddard Space Flight
Center/NASA; 2-3: GSFC/Solar Dynamics Observatory/
NASA; 4-5: GSFC/NASA; 6: Arctic-Images/Getty
Images; 9: JPL-Caltech/STScl/NASA; 11: Mikkel Juul
Jensen/Science Source; 12: SDO/AIA/HMI/Goddard
Space Flight Center/NASA; 13: Goldenkb/Dreamstime;
14-15: Avalon_Studio/iStockphoto; 16: SSC/NASA;
18-19: Magictorch; 20: Yuliia Markova/Shutterstock;
23: Clearviewstock/Dreamstime; 24: NASA; 25: David
Nunuk/Science Source; 26-27: NASA; 28-29: Ken Karp
Photography; 28-29 graph paper: Natbasil/Dreamstime;
28-29 paper clip: Angela Jones/Dreamstime; 30
background: Metthapaul Potinil/Shutterstock; 30 left:
Walt Disney Studios Motion Pictures/Photofest; 30
right: De Agostini/G. Nimatallah/Getty Images; 31
top: Sarunyu_foto/Shutterstock; 31 center top: peepo/
iStockphoto; 31 center bottom, bottom: Magictorch; 32:
Jo Bradford/Green Island Art Studios/Getty Images.

**Scholastic Inc., 557 Broadway,
New York, NY 10012.**

Table of Contents

Let's Explore the Sun!

Each morning, the sun rises into the sky. It is there to greet you when you wake up. On clear days, it looks like a bright circle overhead.

The sun makes life on Earth possible. It gives us light. It keeps us warm. We could not survive without the sun!

I am Rocket. Do you want to explore the universe with me? Then get ready to blast off. Next stop, the sun!

When the sun sets, you can see thousands of other stars from Earth.

A Ball of Fire

Have you ever seen stars twinkling in the night sky? Each star is a giant ball of very hot gases. The sun is a star, too. It looks bigger and brighter than other stars in the sky. That is because the sun is the closest star to Earth. Still, it is millions of miles from our planet.

It would take you 20 years to reach the sun in an airplane.

The sun is about 4.6 billion years old. If formed inside a nebula. That is a huge cloud of gas and dust in space. Over millions of years, **gravity** pulled bits of gas and dust together. They formed a spinning ball. The ball slowly gathered more gas and dust. It grew much bigger and much hotter until it formed our sun.

The sun is a medium-size star. There are other stars that are a thousand times as big!

The sun and other stars form inside nebulas, like this one. It is the Orion Nebula.

The sun is made up mostly of a gas called hydrogen (**hahy**-druh-juhn). The huge weight of the sun tightly squeezes hydrogen in the sun's center. That squeezing pressure causes some of the gas to combine. It forms a new gas called helium (**hee**-lee-uhm). This process gives off a huge amount of **energy**. The sun releases this energy as heat and light.

It takes about eight minutes for light from the sun to reach Earth.

The Sun's Layers

The sun is made up of four main layers.

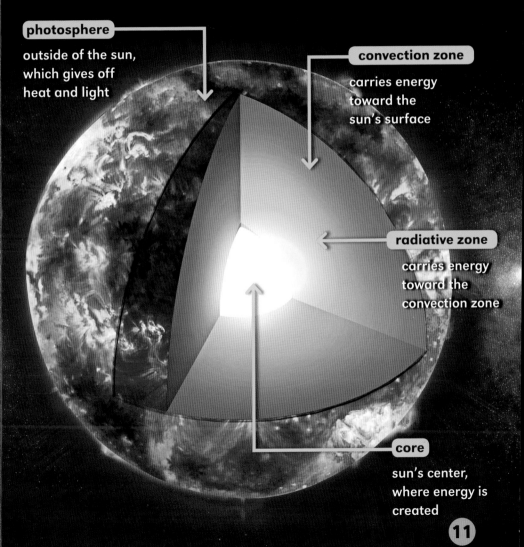

photosphere
outside of the sun, which gives off heat and light

convection zone
carries energy toward the sun's surface

radiative zone
carries energy toward the convection zone

core
sun's center, where energy is created

The surface of the sun is always churning and moving as hot gases bubble up from inside.

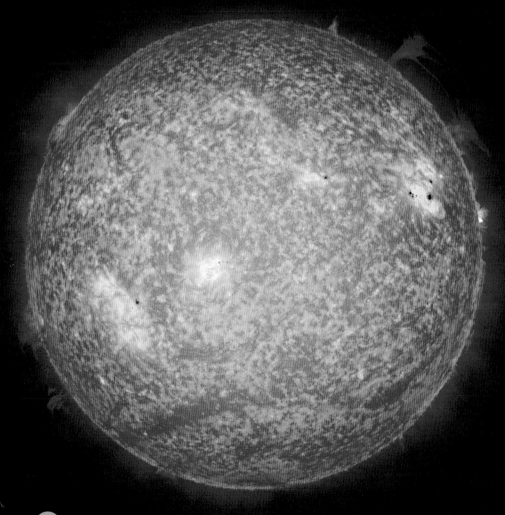

Our yellow sun is only a medium-temperature star. Blue stars are even hotter!

The sun is *really, really* hot. Its outside temperature is about 10,000°F (5,500°C). That is about 20 times as hot as the highest setting on a kitchen oven. The sun's center is even hotter. It reaches about 27 million °F (15 million °C).

Heat from the sun keeps Earth warm—especially in summer!

Burning Bright

Without the sun, there could be no life on Earth. The sun's heat keeps our planet at just the right temperature—not too hot and not too cold. And the sun's light helps plants grow. People and animals rely on plants for food.

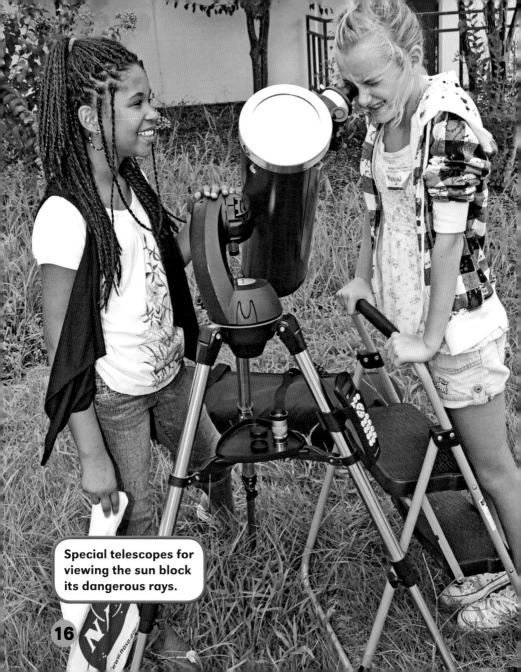

Special telescopes for viewing the sun block its dangerous rays.

The sun's bright rays also have a dangerous side. They are so strong they can harm your eyes. It is never safe to look directly at the sun.

The sun's rays can cause sunburn, too. A sunburn can be very painful. It may also damage your skin.

Wearing sunglasses may help protect your eyes on a sunny day. And sunscreen helps block the sun's harmful rays.

A Star in Space

The sun is the center of our **solar system**. Earth, our home, is one of eight planets that **orbit** the sun. Mercury, Venus, Earth, and Mars are the closest planets to the sun. Jupiter, Saturn, Uranus, and Neptune are farther away.

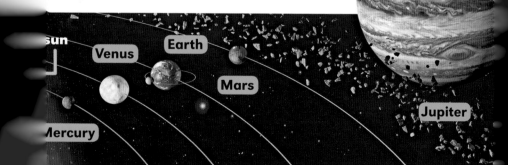

Sun

Venus

Earth

Mars

Jupiter

Mercury

Our solar system is just one of many in space. There may be billions of other stellar systems in the universe.

Neptune

Uranus

Saturn

All eight planets orbit the sun in the same direction.

Just How Big Is the Sun?

This illustration shows how big the sun is compared to the planets in our solar system.

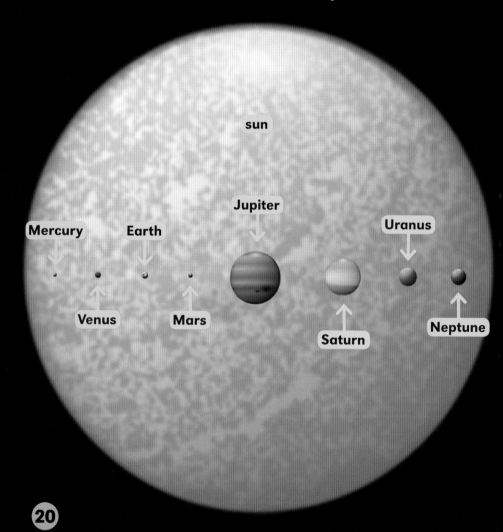

The sun is the biggest object in our solar system. Because the sun is so big, it has lots of gravity. The sun's gravity tugs on the planets as they move through space. The pull of the sun keeps the planets moving around it. Otherwise, the planets would just fly off into space.

The sun is BIG! One million Earths could fit inside it.

Each planet takes a different amount of time to make a complete orbit of the sun. Earth takes 365¼ days—or one year. Each planet also spins as it circles the sun. It takes Earth 24 hours to make one full spin. That equals one day. Other planets spin faster or slower than Earth. That makes their days shorter or longer than ours.

When one side of a planet faces the sun, it is day there. It is night on the other side.

Days and Years Across the Solar System

Here are the lengths of days and years on other planets compared to Earth.

Planet	Length of Day Compared to Earth	Length of Year Compared to Earth
Mercury	1,416 hours	88 days
Venus	5,832 hours	225 days
Earth	24 hours	365 days
Mars	24 hours and 40 minutes	687 days
Jupiter	10 hours	4,380 days
Saturn	10 hours and 39 minutes	10,950 days
Uranus	17 hours	30,660 days
Neptune	16 hours	60,225 days

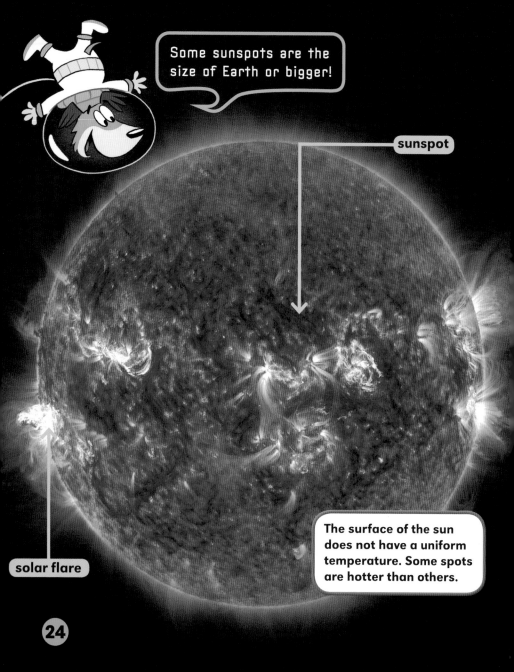

Secrets of the Sun

Scientists have discovered areas on the sun that look dark. They are called sunspots. They are cooler than the rest of the sun's surface. Scientists also see bursts of energy shoot from the sun. They are called solar flares. They can reach billions of miles into space.

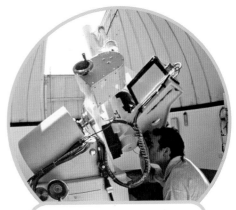

Scientists in Australia use this telescope to monitor activity on the sun.

The STEREO-B spacecraft was launched to take close-up photos of the sun.

Eventually, the sun will use up all of its fuel supply. It will cool and dim. Luckily, that will not happen for about five billion years. Until then, scientists will keep working to learn more about our amazing star.

The warmth of the sun makes me sleepy. Time for a nap!

Investigate Light

Discover the combination of colors in sunlight. Be sure to ask an adult for help!

YOU WILL NEED:

- ✓ Aluminum foil
- ✓ Flashlight
- ✓ Pencil
- ✓ CD
- ✓ Yellow and red cellophane sheets
- ✓ Paper

STEP-BY-STEP:

1

Tear a square of aluminum foil large enough to cover the top of the flashlight. Wrap it over the flashlight.

2

Using the pencil, poke a hole about ⅓ inch (1 centimeter) wide in the center of the foil.

3

In a darkened room, place the CD on a table, label side down. Turn on the flashlight. Point it diagonally at the CD so the light reflects off the CD and into your eyes. Record what you see.

4

Repeat Step 3, but this time hold the yellow cellophane between the flashlight and the CD. Record what you see.

5 Repeat Step 4, but this time hold the red cellophane between the flashlight and the CD. Record what you see.

Think About It:

What colors did you see in Step 3? How did that change in Steps 4 and 5? Why, do you think, did this happen?

Stories About the Sun

The sun is a big part of life on Earth. People have long told stories about our star and tried to learn more about it.

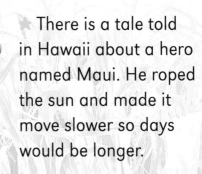

There is a tale told in Hawaii about a hero named Maui. He roped the sun and made it move slower so days would be longer.

For hundreds of years, it was believed that the sun circled Earth. In 1543, scientist Nicolaus Copernicus argued that the opposite is true.

Glossary

energy (**en**-ur-jee): power in forms such as heat, light, and motion

gravity (**grav**-ih-tee): force that pulls things toward each other; there is very little gravity in space

orbit (**or**-bit): travel in a circular path around a planet or the sun

solar system (**soh**-lur **siss**-tuhm): the sun and all the objects that travel around it

Index

Facts for Now

Visit this Scholastic Web site for more information
on the sun:

www.factsfornow.scholastic.com

Enter the keyword Sun

About the Author

Cody Crane is an award-winning nonfiction children's writer. From a young age, she was set on becoming a scientist. She later discovered that writing about science could be just as fun as the real thing. She lives in Houston, Texas, with her husband and son.